cl🍀verleaf books™

Space Adventures

To the Moon!

Jodie Shepherd

illustrated by Mike Byrne

M MILLBROOK PRESS • MINNEAPOLIS

For curious kids everywhere—J.S.

For Jareth—M.B.

Millbrook Press
A division of Lerner Publishing Group, Inc.
241 First Avenue North
Minneapolis, MN 55401 USA

For reading levels and more information, look up this title at
www.lernerbooks.com.

Main body text set in Slappy Inline 22/28.
Typeface provided by T26.

Library of Congress Cataloging-in-Publication Data

Names: Shepherd, Jodie.
Title: To the moon! / Jodie Shepherd ; illustrated by Mike Byrne.
Description: Minneapolis : Millbrook Press, [2017] | Series:
    Cloverleaf books. Space adventures | Audience: Age 5–8. |
    Audience: K to grade 3. | Includes index. | Description based
    on print version record and CIP data provided by publisher;
    resource not viewed.
Identifiers: LCCN 2016019255 (print) | LCCN
    2016012589 (ebook) | ISBN 9781512428339 (eb pdf) |
    ISBN 9781512425369 (lb : alk. paper) | ISBN 9781512430851
    (pb : alk. paper)
Subjects: LCSH: Moon—Exploration—Juvenile literature. | Lunar
    geology—Juvenile literature.
Classification: LCC QB582 (print) | LCC QB582 .S5345 2017
    (ebook) | DDC 629.45/4—dc23

LC record available at https://lccn.loc.gov/2016019255

Manufactured in the United States of America
1-41304-23248-8/16/2016

TABLE OF CONTENTS

Chapter One

Astronaut Neil Strong

"Hey, that's almost *my* name!" Neil shouted. He was at the Space Museum with his class. In front of him was a photo of the first person on the moon: Neil Armstrong.

ONE SMALL STEP FOR [A] MAN, ONE GIANT LEAP FOR MANKIND —NEIL ARMSTRONG

"Awesome!" Neil exclaimed. "Someday it's going to be me, Neil *Strong*, who walks on the moon."

The spacecraft *Apollo 11* carried Neil Armstrong and two other astronauts to the moon on July 20, 1969. The world watched on TV as Neil Armstrong stepped onto the moon.

ONE SMALL STEP
FOR [A] MAN,
ONE GIANT LEAP
FOR MANKIND
—NEIL ARMSTRONG

"Astronauts last visited the moon in 1972," said Neil's teacher, Ms. Pelusa. "But scientists are talking about making moon landings again— with human astronauts or maybe with androids. It could happen in the next ten years."

Neil read a sign: "The moon is about 240,000 miles away. It's the only other place in our universe where humans have stood."

"That's amazing!" Neil said.

HUMANS WERE HERE!

An android is a robot that can move around like a person. Android bodies usually look similar to human bodies.

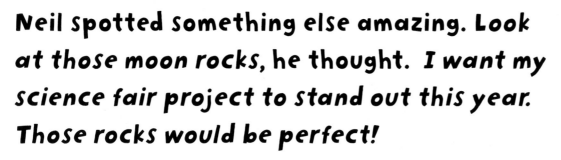

Neil spotted something else amazing. Look at those moon rocks, he thought. *I want my science fair project to stand out this year. Those rocks would be perfect!*

Neil sighed. *I can't take the rocks with me. They belong to the museum. If only I could go to the moon and get rocks of my own!*

Suddenly Neil noticed a model of Apollo 11 nearby. He sat at the controls. *Maybe if I use my imagination . . .* And then, before he knew it . . . **LIFTOFF!**

Billions of years ago, an object about the size of Mars crashed into Earth. Chunks of rock broke off from Earth and later formed the moon.

Chapter Two

Luna

Astronaut Neil has landed on the moon! He gasped in wonder.

The moon was amazing! And there was someone else there with him too—an android.

"I am Luna," it said. "Welcome to the moon! Good thing you wore your space suit. The moon gets burning hot and freezing cold. And it has almost no air. Your space helmet gives you oxygen to breathe."

From Earth, the moon appears to change shape. But it does not. We just see different amounts of the moon. What we see depends on where the sun, moon, and Earth are in the sky.

There was a lot to see—mountains and hills and . . . "Are those oceans?" Neil asked.

"They *look* like oceans," Luna answered. "But they are large fields filled with dark, solid lava."

Since the moon has very little air, there's no sound up there. Astronauts must talk to one another on radios inside their air-filled helmets.

Neil spotted a lava rock. He stopped to pick it up for his science fair project. Then he saw footprints! Who could have made them?

Chapter Three

Boing!

Luna saw the surprise on Neil's face. "Do not worry. Those are Neil Armstrong's footprints," Luna explained. "There is no wind on the moon. So Neil's footprints may last for millions of years!"

Astronauts from the United States have brought US flags to the moon. All but one of the flags are still standing! *Apollo 11* knocked over its flag when it lifted off.

My footprints will last too, Neil thought. I'll be famous forever!

He picked up a second rock. His science project was going to *rock*!

Walking wasn't easy on the moon.
But bouncing was!

If you weigh
50 pounds (23
kilograms) on Earth,
you'll weigh just over
8 pounds (4 kg) on
the moon.

"The moon has very little gravity," Luna told him. "On Earth, gravity holds people and other things to the ground. Since the moon has less gravity, you weigh less here."

Boingy! Boingy! Jumping on the moon was fun!

Neil saw craters everywhere. Some were huge. Others looked like large soup bowls. "What made these craters?" Neil asked Luna, putting another rock in his backpack.

The biggest moon crater is about 1,500 miles (2,414 km) from side to side—more than half the width of the United States! The smallest moon craters are 1 inch (2.5 centimeters) wide.

"Meteors crashing into the moon made craters on the moon's surface," Luna said. "Now turn around and take a look at Earthrise. Amazing, is it not?"

Earthrise *was* amazing, but it made Neil really homesick.

Chapter Four
Back on Earth

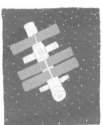

ONE SMALL STE[P]
FOR [A] MAN,
ONE GIANT LEA[P]
FOR MANKIND
—NEIL ARMSTRO[NG]

Poof! Just like that, Neil was back at the museum. But he didn't have any rocks. He had imagined the entire mission! Still, he'd learned lots of cool facts about the moon.

Neil knew how he could make his science fair project stand out. He'd share everything he'd learned. And he'd look up awesome pictures of the moon to show off at the fair. *Even better*, Neil thought, *Someday I'll go to the moon for real!*

Make a Moon Diary

What You Will Need

a sketchbook or notebook
a pencil, a pen, or colored markers or crayons

How to Make Your Moon Diary

Go outside each night and look at the moon. Draw what you see!
How many days does it take for the moon to change from the
crescent shape to the full moon and back again? Pretend to be a
werewolf and howl at the full moon!

android: a robot that resembles a human

crater: a large hole on the surface of a planet or the moon

gravity: the force that holds objects to Earth or other bodies in space and that keeps things from drifting away

meteor: a small body of material from outer space

oxygen: a gas found in both water and air that humans and other animals need to live and breathe

BOOKS

Bellisario, Gina. *To Mars!* Minneapolis: Millbrook Press, 2017. Come along with Avery as she takes a trip to Mars!

Salas, Laura Purdie. *If You Were the Moon.* Minneapolis: Millbrook Press, 2017. This picture book poetically explores the many different roles the moon plays.

Scott, Elaine. *Our Moon: New Discoveries about Earth's Closest Companion.* Boston: Clarion Books, 2015. This book includes the most up-to-date information about the moon—such as details about the moon's atmosphere and the presence of frozen water.

WEBSITES

Enchanted Learning: All about Our Solar System
http://www.enchantedlearning.com/subjects/astronomy/solarsystem
Read about our solar system and find fun space-related activities.

Kids Astronomy
http://kidsastronomy.com
Learn about the solar system, space exploration, and the universe at this website.

NASA: The Moon
http://www.nasa.gov/moon
Learn moon basics, see cool photos, and more at this site from NASA.

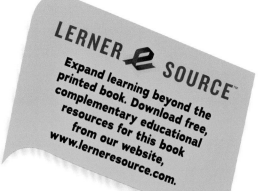

LERNER 𝓮 SOURCE™

Expand learning beyond the printed book. Download free, complementary educational resources for this book from our website, www.lerneresource.com.